The First American Flag

by Kathy Allen
illustrated by Siri Weber Feeney

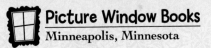

Picture Window Books
Minneapolis, Minnesota

Special thanks to our advisers for their expertise:

Susanna Robbins, M.A.
Former Assistant Editor, OAH Magazine of History
Terry Flaherty, Ph.D., Professor of English
Minnesota State University, Mankato

Editor: Jill Kalz
Designer: Abbey Fitzgerald
Page Production: Melissa Kes
Art Director: Nathan Gassman
Editorial Director: Nick Healy
Creative Director: Joe Ewest
The illustrations in this book were created with acrylic paint and colored pencil.

Photo Credits: cover (leather texture), Shutterstock/Leigh Prather; 2 (parchment texture), Shutterstock/AGA

Picture Window Books
151 Good Counsel Drive
P.O. Box 669
Mankato, MN 56002-0669
877-845-8392
www.picturewindowbooks.com

All books published by Picture Window Books
are manufactured with paper containing at least
10 percent post-consumer waste.

Library of Congress Cataloging-in-Publication Data
Allen, Kathy.
The first American flag / by Kathy Allen ; illustrated by Siri Weber Feeney.
p. cm. — (Our American story)
Includes index.
ISBN 978-1-4048-5541-0 (library binding)
1. Flags—United States—Juvenile literature. I. Feeney, Siri Weber, ill. II. Title.
CR113.A825 2010
929.9'20973—dc22
                                                    2009006892

Do you know the legend of Betsy Ross?

Betsy was a seamstress. She sewed all sorts of things. The legend says she sewed something special one day in 1776. It was the first flag of the United States. But that story is not true.

At that time, the American colonies belonged to
Great Britain. The Colonists thought King George III
and the British government were treating them unfairly.

The Colonists wanted to rule themselves. They wanted their own country. In 1775, they went to war to be free.

When the Revolutionary War began,
the British flag flew over the Colonies.

The flag had red and white stripes
on a blue background.

The Colonists wanted their own country. They needed their own flag, too. So they began to fly a new flag.

It had red, white, and blue in the corner. Thirteen red and white stripes stood for the 13 Colonies.

No one knows who made this flag. But the Colonists thought it looked too much like the flag of Great Britain.

In the legend of Betsy Ross, George Washington and two other men came to Betsy's home. It was June 1776. They showed her a drawing of stars and stripes and asked her to sew a new flag. Betsy quickly went to work.

But this is just a story. No proof shows the meeting happened. Betsy did make flags. But she didn't make the first one. Many people believe a man named Francis Hopkinson designed the first U.S. flag.

His flag had 13 red and white stripes. The corner had 13 six-pointed stars on a patch of blue.

On June 14, 1777, "Hopkinson's flag" became the first flag of the United States. It was called the Stars and Stripes.

When the Colonists won the war, they flew this flag. The United States was a free country, and it had its own flag.

Different flag makers sewed their own Stars and Stripes. Some made stars with five points. Some made stars with six, seven, or eight points. Flags appeared in different sizes.

As states were added to the country, stars and stripes were added to the flag. By 1795, the flag had 15 stars and 15 stripes.

This flag flew in a new war with Great Britain. The war was called the War of 1812.

In September 1814, a battle raged at a U.S. fort called Fort McHenry. British soldiers bombed the fort all night. It looked like the Americans would lose.

But the next morning, the U.S. flag continued to fly. An American named Francis Scott Key saw it. He knew the United States had won. He wrote about the flag in a poem called "The Star-Spangled Banner."

Oh, say, can you see, by the dawn's early light,

What so proudly we hail'd at the twilight's last gleaming?

Whose broad stripes and bright stars, thro' the perilous fight,

O'er the ramparts we watch'd, were so gallantly streaming? ...

By 1818, there were 20 states.

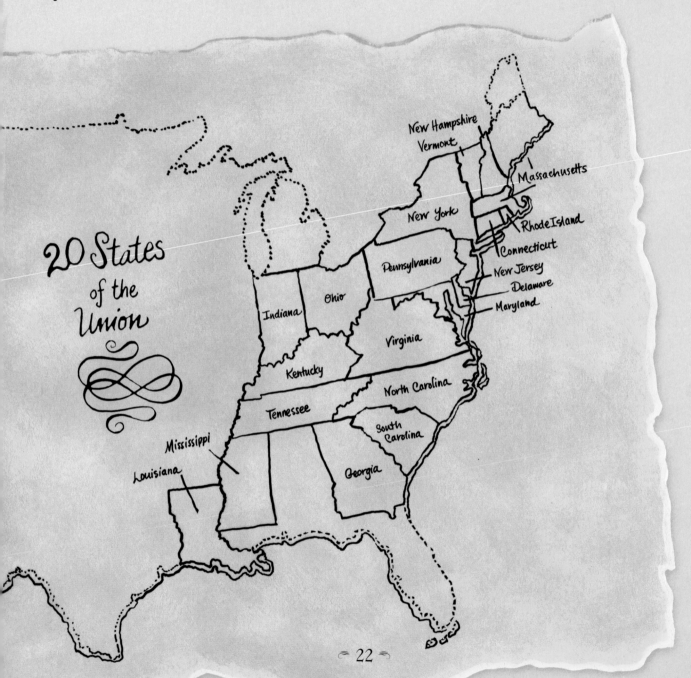

20 States
of the
Union

New Hampshire
Vermont
Massachusetts
New York
Rhode Island
Connecticut
New Jersey
Pennsylvania
Delaware
Maryland
Indiana
Ohio
Virginia
Kentucky
North Carolina
Tennessee
South Carolina
Mississippi
Louisiana
Georgia

Adding a new stripe for each new state would mean very small stripes or a very tall flag!

So, the country went back to a flag with 13 stripes. A star was added for each new state.

The U.S. flag needed to look the same throughout the country. The size of the flag became law in the early 1900s. Stars were soon set in rows.

By 1912, there were 48 states, and 48 stars. The United States flew this flag during World War II.

By 1959, there were 50 states. The flag got its 50th star on July 4, 1960. The star stands for the state of Hawaii.

Astronauts planted this flag on the moon in 1969.

The United States is a land of many different people with many different ideas. For more than 200 years, the U.S. flag has stood for all of them.

The flag of the United States has
come a long way since 1776.

Timeline

1776	—	Congress approves the Declaration of Independence on July 4.
1777	—	Congress passes the First Flag Act, creating the first Stars and Stripes.
1781	—	British soldiers surrender at Yorktown, Virginia, on October 19. Peace agreement signed two years later.
1794	—	Congress passes the Second Flag Act, adding two stars and two stripes.
1814	—	Francis Scott Key sees the flag at Fort McHenry on September 14 and writes a poem called "The Star-Spangled Banner."
1818	—	Congress passes the Third Flag Act, returning the flag to 13 stripes, with a star added for each new state.
1960	—	The 50th star is added to the U.S. flag.

Glossary

approves—gives the official OK

colonies / Colonies—lands ruled by another country; the 13 British colonies that became the United States

colonists / Colonists—people who live in a colony; the people who lived in the 13 Colonies

Congress—the group of people in the U.S. government who make laws

Declaration of Independence—a document (paper) that says the United States is a free country and every U.S. citizen has rights that the government should protect

legend—a story passed down through the years that many people believe but which may not be entirely true

proof—facts that show something is true

Revolutionary War—(1775–1783) the American colonies' fight against Great Britain for freedom

seamstress—a woman who sews

War of 1812—(1812–1815) the war between the United States and Great Britain over unfair British control of shipping

World War II—(1939–1945) the war fought between the United States, Great Britain, France, and the Soviet Union against Germany, Japan, and Italy

To Learn More

∞ More Books to Read ∞

→ Firestone, Mary. *Our American Flag.* Minneapolis: Picture Window Books, 2007.

→ Hicks, Kelli L. *The American Flag.* Vero Beach, Fla.: Rourke Pub., 2009.

→ Landau, Elaine. *The American Flag.* New York: Children's Press, 2008.

→ Thomson, Sarah L. *American Flag Q&A.* New York: Collins, 2008.

∞ Internet Sites ∞

FactHound offers a safe, fun way to find Internet sites related to this book. All of the sites on FactHound have been researched by our staff.

Here's all you do:

Visit *www.facthound.com*

FactHound will fetch the best sites for you!

Look for all of the books in the Our American Story series:

→ The First American Flag

→ Paul Revere's Ride

→ President George Washington

→ Writing the U.S. Constitution